BETTER GYMNASTICS

Pauline Prestidge

Better Gymnastics

Photographs by Jim Prestidge

Kaye & Ward · London
in association with Methuen of Australia
and Hicks, Smith & Sons, New Zealand

First published by
Kaye & Ward Ltd
21 New Street, London EC2M 4NT
1977
Reprinted 1978

Copyright © Kaye & Ward Ltd 1977

All Rights Reserved. No part of this publication may be
reproduced, stored in a retrieval system, or transmitted,
in any form or by any means, electronic, mechanical, photocopying
recording or otherwise, without the prior permission of the
copyright owner.

ISBN 0 7182 1450 1

Photoset in Monophoto Univers by Computer Photoset Ltd, Birmingham
Printed in Great Britain by Cox & Wyman Ltd, London, Fakenham and Reading

Contents

Introduction	7
Body Preparation	13
Acrobatics and Tumbling Skills	20
The Asymmetric Bars	47
Vaulting	76
The Beam	84

Introduction

This book is about Gymnastics, and how best to succeed in the sport. We have all seen and witnessed on television the incredible skills of young girls, and not quite such young boys. Perhaps many reading these words are young and would like to emulate their achievements — and why not? — The sport offers so much.

In the environment of a gym club, one can find so many things — enjoyment, excitement, challenge, satisfaction, friendship, and sometimes disappointment. All these feelings and emotions are essential for success, for they bring out the necessary qualities of dedication, skill and courage needed for the sport. The skills of gymnastics are not easily achieved nor in the achieving are they without pain and frustration. They are the result of many years training, of performing and repeating simple exercises many, many times.

Gymnastics is no different from the practice of any other art form — perfection of the simple rules and basic exercises make for a perfect performance.

A planned progressive programme of exercising and body preparation is vital — but in addition, gymnastics requires that extra something in the way of will power to sustain the arduous task of repeating simple elements many, many times and for a long period of time. Physical talent alone does not make a world champion!

But it is primarily the gymnast's own attitude and realisation of the need to spend many hours preparing the body so that it is strong and supple and skill orientated. To discipline their daily practice of the basic skills until they are perfect. Only this personal effort (together with a coach to guide) will achieve success.

Display night for the Ladywell Club.

Fun Gymnastics for T.V.'s Sports Personalities programme, filmed at the Crystal Palace.

There is no glamour in the first years of learning, but a great sense of fun coupled with a simple satisfaction. It is here that the qualities of the coach are so important. A class of beginners taking their first hesitant step is just as important as a group of national class gymnasts. Fun and enjoyment, tempered with the simple disciplines, are the essence of good gymnastics.

This need for body preparation must be fully understood and appreciated by the coach and gymnast. Some perhaps would ignore the boring procedure of exercise and see no purpose in progressive skill learning — on the contrary, without careful and prolonged body preparation and without a slow build-up of skill techniques, with psychological aids to progression, especially into the very complex skills — one cannot hope for, nor will one achieve success.

Without this preparation the body would be unable to achieve the extended and extremely supple shapes required, and the mind would not be orientated to allow the body to plunge backwards or forwards into space, or to twist and turn whilst in flight.

Throughout all stages of learning, there must be preparation and breakdown of skills.

One can begin to use this method of teaching from a very young age — children at five years and younger enjoy swinging, jumping and rolling on apparatus that is modified to suit their heights and capabilities. They enjoy, too, performing exercises to music. Basic ballet exercises are all a vital part of training and enjoyable. The Tendué (stretching the leg with extended ankle), the Plié (bending the knees), Port de bras (carriage of the head and arms), all these basic ballet exercises should be included in the lesson plan. Simple dance steps and game activities which include running and jumping can all be included to make enjoyable and exciting sessions. At the same time, this will be increasing the strength and suppleness of the body.

The sessions for the 'Under 5's' which are very popular in our Sports Centre, are the first steps towards this approach. The children, boys and girls, play freely on gymnastic apparatus, and are already getting the 'feel' of things. Every piece of apparatus is placed in a safe and suitable position — and erected at heights suited to this young age group.

The Battment Tendu.

The Demi Plie.

The Full Plie.

Hop Springs. The 2nd and 4th gymnast from the right of the picture are technically correct, showing good use of legs, shoulders relaxed, and good body alignment.

Where it all begins! The under 5's.

FIRST THE EXERCISE THEN THE WHOLE SKILL!

This progressive approach to gymnastic skill learning and the body preparation is essential both for the elite gymnast and for the recreational level. In the latter case, it is the only possible solution to coping with large numbers of children in a class situation.

All skills are made up of a combination of body shapes and forces and if each skill is analysed and the fundamental shapes or actions are practised many times, then the whole skill will be achieved more easily and with greater perfection. In this approach, all levels of ability will have some success.

An intelligent understanding by the coach is necessary in order to apply this method of teaching. Wherever possible, create safe situations by adjusting the height or type of apparatus, using soft mats for landings.

This book will deal throughout its pages with this approach in mind. Each section of the gymanstic programme will be treated in the same way — first the exercise, then the whole skill.

Body Preparation

All forms of movement, whether it be through art, sport or recreation, require some body preparation. It is essential to warm-up to the activity to be performed, not only to increase the blood circulation, thereby reducing the risk of pulled muscles and strained tendons, but as a psychological aid to mobilise the mind and body to accept that movement. In gymnastics, it is essential to be very supple in all parts of the body. It is equally important to be strong, especially in the shoulders, legs, arms, stomach and back. This condition is not a natural physical state, and can only be achieved by correct repetitive exercising.

It is also very important that the coach should understand how the body functions in order to correct alignment of legs, pelvis and shoulders. Body tension and relaxation too must be practised. It is not possible to jump from the hands, as in the handspring, without body tension. It is equally impossible to perform fluid expressive movements of dance without some relaxation.

A correct body stance is essential — feet firmly placed on the ground without any outward or inward rotation, straight legs, pressing the backs of the legs towards each other and tightening the muscles of the bottom; stomach muscles contracted, and the back straight; the shoulders relaxed and the neck extended with the head in normal line with the spine.

All the body positions and shapes whether static or moving should derive from the basic correct stance. The balance on the hands should be exactly the same as the balance on the feet only in reverse, the hands taking over the work of the feet. The head should be in line with the spine, the pelvis pulled in and the back straight. There must be no 'hollow' i.e. bending of the back as was once thought to be ideal for the handstand.

Young gymnasts learning the art form of gymnastics — upper body relaxation and expression.

When bending forwards, sideways or backwards, the body must first take this correct stance and then bend by extending and not by sagging. Back bends should begin in the top of the spine and move down the spine as the bend increases.

When swinging the legs through lifted positions during ballet exercises, the hips should not 'roll' or 'twist'. The supporting leg should be held straight and the foot remain firm on the ground.

When arms are swinging or lifting, the body should remain in correct stance and the arms rotate in the joints.

Incorrect stance — but commonly seen in the young child.

Correct body stance, a very essential body posture for the gymnast.

Ankle and leg extension. Ensure that the long sitting position is correct with body weight 'sitting' on the upper leg, stomach muscles contracted, spine straight. Press the backs of the legs to the floor whilst flexing and stretching the ankles.

Grande Battments, an exercise for leg strength and hip mobility — keep the supporting leg straight and body upright.

An exercise for extra suppleness in the legs.

Hip and leg mobility exercise. Note that the younger gymnasts in the front of the picture are not yet aware of correct leg alignment. The legs are rolling inwards!

Leg lifts for increasing tension in seat and legs.

Back strengthening exercises. Position can also be held for X number of seconds to improve body tension.

Prone support — the correct position for commencement of 'press-ups'. The arms should bend and the body lower almost touching the floor. Body must remain straight with tension in seat and stomach muscles.

'The Leaning Tower' activity for body tension awareness. The body during the 'lean' should retain complete tension without bending in the back or creating angles at hip and shoulder joints.

Body Shapes — the straight and extended body. The middle spine should be pressed to the floor, arms and shoulders touching the floor. This same body shape is correct for handstands, jumps, long swings etc.

The Bridge. It is essential to understand that the straight legs are not achieved by moving the feet away from the hands! The aim is to increase the mobility in the shoulders and back by pushing downwards and backwards through the feet; arms should be straight.

The Tuck position as in all rolling actions and tucked somersaults.

Ankles must be exercised, flexing and stretching to the maximum. Toes and ankles must be strong.

A programme of basic classical ballet exercises are very valuable and give strength to the feet and legs. Typical exercises for the essential areas of the body that need mobility and strength are shown in the photographs. In each chapter of the book and for certain skills, you will find additional exercises especially for those skills.

Body shapes should also be taught as part of the preparative period in the class lesson. All gymnastic skills are made up of a comparatively small number of body shapes, i.e. the hollow or hyperextended body; the pike; the tuck; the bend or bridge; the straddle. It is vital to feel these 'shapes' during the early training or class lesson, for the gymnast must make rapid changes of body shapes during the performances of skills.

One does not become strong or supple simply by performing skills, but only through the practising of exercises which strengthen and mobilise each and every part of the body. As the gymnast develops and the level of performance increases, so too should the exercising increase either by more repetitions or by increasing the force behind the exercise.

There are many exercises that help to develop these body requirements, too many to describe in this book unfortunately. But there is a simple guide line or rule by which one should work. Wherever strength or suppleness is required, then that part of the body should receive more exercise. Having performed 'X' number of legswings or press-ups, the muscles should then feel tired and the limbs loose — if so, then obviously the exercise is having some effect.

Be sure when practising the strength and mobility exercises that the basic rule of good body posture and alignment are maintained throughout.

Never strengthen or stretch limbs and joints when the body is cold — every part of the body must be thoroughly warm beforehand.

Acrobatics and Tumbling Skills

The skills of acrobatics and tumbling are the first that we learn in gymnastics for the simple reason that they form the basis of all other skills on apparatus. In addition, of course, no other hazard exists when working at ground level – the floor can be cushioned and one cannot fall far! Having mastered the skills in this 'safe' situation, then many of them can be easily adapted for performance on the apparatus. Never attempt a skill for the first time on apparatus until it can be performed with certainty on the floor, or at least in a position which is made safe by virtue of the fact that you perform it at a lower level or on a wider base.

Each skill described in this book will be preceded by the 'skill activity', that is, the practice of part or all of the skill in a simpler form. Many such activities can be included in the class teaching situation during the preparation period, and especially so if there is little or no apparatus.

When one is ready to advance to apparatus, then the approach should be in the same way. With this type of 'build-up' to the advanced skills, one is not only approaching the movement in the correct and safest way, but one is enabling those gymnasts of lesser ability to experience the sensation of near performance.

THE FORWARD AND BACKWARD ROLL

Skill Exercise – Rolling and Tucking

The spine must be completely curved with the head forward, chin to chest. The rolling backwards begins from the sitting position. The stomach muscles should be contracted, and the roll, with the hands in a position to touch the floor behind the head in line with the shoulders, must

The roll to the shoulders with correct hand placement.

Returning forward to the half standing position.

The Backward Roll to straddle stand, a useful skill for leg extension practice. Slide the feet away pressing downwards.

continue until only the upper spine remains in contact with the floor. Allow the roll to return forwards sufficiently for the body to lift from the floor. To assist this 'half standing' position, keep the shoulders and head forwards, arms outstretched in front of the body.

Repeat the rolling action many times, changing the leg shape both in the forward and backward roll. Legs can be straight; straddled; each leg can take a different shape, one bent, one straight etc.

The Forward Roll

From the standing position, bend the knees keeping the back straight, place the hands forward on to the floor and at the same time thrust from the floor with the feet, straightening the legs so that the hips lift. Tuck the head and allow only the shoulders to make first contact with the floor. Continue to roll, curving the back, coming to the feet as in the preparation rolling exercise.

The Backward Roll

This can also begin from the standing position. Crouch as before and begin to roll as in the skill exercise. The back and hip lift will assist the roll to the feet, together with the push from the hands. The legs as stated, may take any shape. It is usual to begin with the legs together and bent.

Very young children learning the backward roll for the first time may be a little apprehensive of going backwards and will flatten the back and therefore cannot roll. Assist the reluctant ones by raising a flat board – the Reuther board will do – so that it is very slightly sloping downwards, cover with a mat and sit the child at the top of the board with knees tucked and hands ready to make contact with the floor, chin to chest. Tell the child to roll backwards. Because the action is speeded up, there is no time to resist, and the 'fear' barrier is broken!

The forward and backward roll should now be practised in sequence form, two or three repetitions in continuous rhythm along a mat.

DEVELOPMENT OF THE FORWARD ROLL

1. Rolling and Jumping

Roll as before, when the feet make contact with the floor, thrust downwards, stretching the knees and ankles and swinging arms forwards and upwards to jump with straight body into the air. Land to bend knees and ankles and roll forward and repeat several times.

Basic position for the start of the forward roll.

The roll.

The straight jump following the roll.

The full turn jump following the roll.

2. Forward Rolls followed by a full turn jump

Roll as before, thrusting from the feet into the stretched jump with the arms swinging forwards and upwards. Keep the arms in line with the head during the turn which is initiated from the toes, hips and shoulders following. Repeat three or four times.

Rolling Activities for Suppling and Strengthening

Backward Rolling

1. Begin the roll by sitting on the floor with straight legs forward and together. Lift the legs from the floor *keeping them straight.* Roll backwards, parting or straddling the legs when the hips are high. Place the feet in a wide straddle on to the floor after the roll. Keep the hands in contact with the floor and slide the legs further out to wide splits. Sit back and repeat again.

2. Roll backwards into the handstand position. Be very conscious of the contraction in the stomach muscles at the beginning of the roll and keep the pelvis lifting throughout. A controlled balance should be achieved on the hands, legs should be kept straight throughout the movement and head in line with spine.

Forward Rolling

1. Begin the roll as for the basic skill. When the middle of the spine has made contact with the floor, straddle the legs, and placing feet firmly on to the ground as the roll continues, place the hands between the legs on to the floor. Pike the body, lifting the hips and finishing in a straddle standing position, hands on floor.

2. Progress still further, when the legs are stronger and the suppleness in the hip increases, attempt to stand without the aid of the hands.

3. Yet another progression producing and requiring strength in stomach, back and shoulders and mobility in hip joints. Begin as for the forward roll to straddle with hands on the floor between the legs, but do not allow

Overcoming the apprehension of the first backward movement. The increased speed of the backward roll down the slightly sloping platform aids its completion to the feet.

the feet to touch the floor at all during the roll! When there is maximum strength and mobility the gymnast should be able to keep the straddled legs lifting into a handstand from the roll!

N.B. The following activities are intended for the more advanced gymanst and should not be taught until the gymnast has good co-ordination and body tension.

FORWARD SOMERSAULT — TAKE-OFF PRACTICE

Skill Activity with Reuther Board and Crash Mat

Place a crash mat in front of the Reuther board (this is a type of spring board). Approach with two or three running steps, taking off from two feet near the top of the board. Swing the arms forwards and upwards on the jump to land on the feet again standing on the crash mat. The arm swing must have correct co-ordination with the take-off jump. Arms must be upwards slightly in front of the head when the body is in flight. The body and legs must be fully stretched with contraction of stomach, seat and leg muscles.

(right) The straight jump showing good technique, arms swinging forwards and upwards on take-off.

(left) The tucked somersault — forwards.

The forward roll keeping the feet from touching the ground. Hips must lift and the body weight must be forwards and taken on the hands.

Dive Roll — Skill Activity with Reuther Board and Crash Mat

Approach as before with two or three running steps, swinging the arms forwards and upwards on take-off, lift the legs backwards and upwards reaching forward for the mat with the hands taking your weight on the hands to roll forwards.

Forward Somersault — with Reuther Board and Crash Mat

As confidence grows and style and technique improves, take off as before with powerful jump, hips moving backwards and upwards, knees bending under the body, head forward to chest, arms coming downwards close to body. Body extends again into the straight position for landing after the tuck.

At first the landing will probably be onto the back or seat — hence the need for a crash mat, but as awareness of the movement becomes more familiar, so the timing of the tuck and the stretch will be felt and understood.

(left) The jump from the box into the trampette, arms down.

(middle) The straight jump out of the trampette arms swinging upwards.

(right) The tucked somersault — forwards.

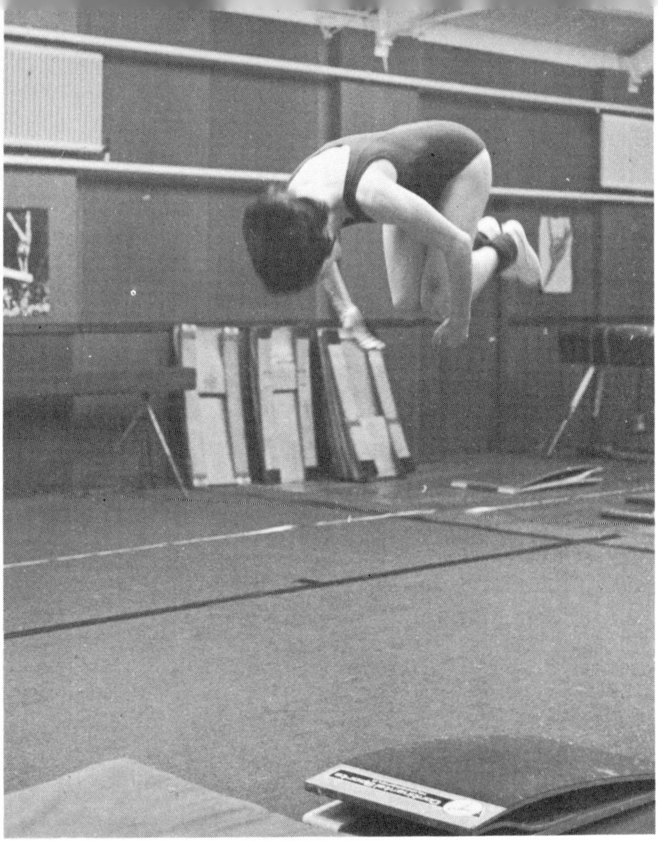
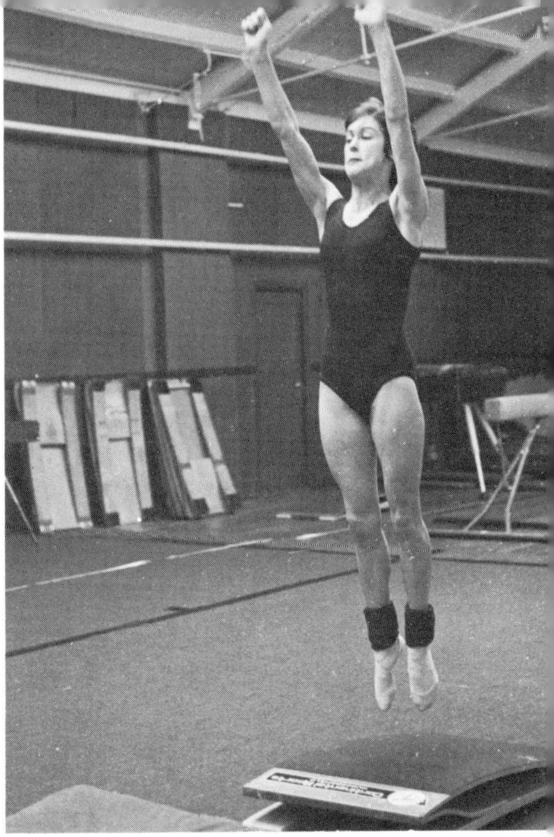
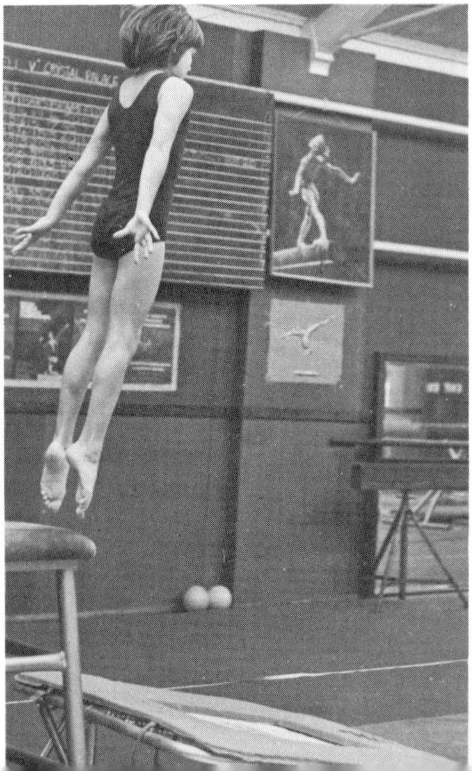
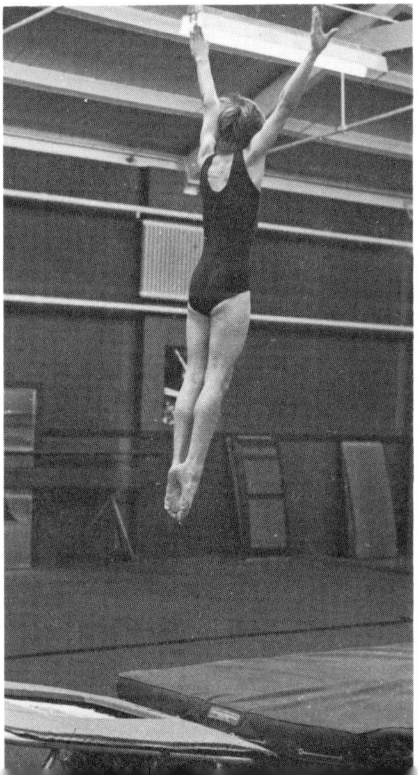
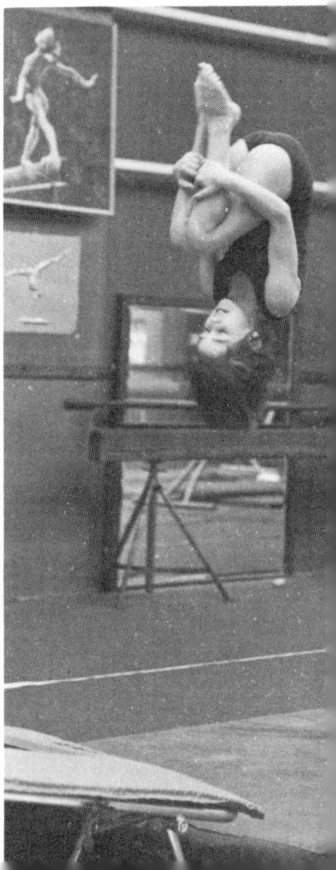

Aim for height in the take-off. This will be achieved by the strong thusting action of the legs and feet from the board with correct and co-ordinated arm swing, body in tension, stomach muscles contracted.

THE FORWARD SOMERSAULT

Skill Activity with Trampette and Crash Mat

The second illustrated somersault activity is equally valuable for awareness and assistance in performing the skill, but may be found to be more difficult. Using a trampette for the first time requires greater body control in flight and more confidence.

Drop from the box top to the trampette, arms downwards on the descent. The body must be full stretched on the rebound arms stretched overhead before lifting the hips and tucking the head. Tuck close, legs folded back under seat, head forward, arms around legs. Open out with full extension of body and legs and stretch the arms upwards overhead to land with feet slightly apart.

THE BACKWARD SOMERSAULT

Orientation for Somersault

Look at the photograph on page 18. It shows the stretched body and the tuck position required for the Backward Somersault. Be familiar with this body shape before making any attempt to somersault.

Now look at the photographs on the next page—this activity will make you familiar with being in the air. Supporters are standing on three layers of boxes. The first photo shows the straight jump, the gymnast being assisted in the jump. Photo 2 shows the tuck position. Aim to swing the hips forwards into the tuck. Photo 3 shows the somersault to land unaided onto the crash mat.

Skill Activity – with Trampette Crash Mat and High Box

Each part of this skill activity has great value for the gymnast. The jump up into the handstand from trampette to box top requires good use of

This supported activity is ideal for height awareness in the backward somersault. Repeat the straight jump at least three times. The gymnast must achieve height by thrusting strongly downwards with the legs.

Swing the hips forwards into the tuck.

Do not lose height on the jump when performing the complete movement.

legs, stomach and back, thus adding strength. The technique of the jump to handstand can be carried through to the Beam and Bars.

The stretched body position in flight must be emphasised and should be practised many times before the tuck is attempted. Do not throw the head backwards into the tuck. The legs must move forwards and upwards, hips and chest lifting into the tuck. Open out with full body and leg extension, stretching the arms up overhead to land with feet slightly apart.

Jump into the trampette from the crash mat. Pike or tuck into the handstand, hands on end of box top.

The handstand position.

Bounce back into the trampette swinging the arms upwards on the jump. Keep good body tension and repeat the jump many times before attempting the backward somersault.

The straight backward Somersault.

When the tucked Somi has been achieved with good technique, then the body shape can be changed to:

(a) a straight position
(b) a pike
(c) straight with a half twist
(d) straight with a full twist

Again it must be thoroughly understood that the vital and most important requirement in the somersault is the upward jump, with good body tension, stomach muscles contracted.

The spring board and trampette are aiding this upward jump and enabling the gymnast to experience the somersaults before they are capable of jumping from the floor. The situation is 'safe' if carefully supervised and very enjoyable for the performer.

Important Note But never perform any of these somersault skills without the supervision of your coach or teacher.

THE HANDSTAND

The Handstand is the gymnast's 'life line'. All progress is dependent upon being able to perform a good hand balance with all parts of the body in line with the point of balance. Early awareness of the middle area of the body is important. The balance on the hands must have the same controlled posture as when standing on the feet. Full use should be made of the hand position on the floor with the weight evenly spread throughout fingers and base of the hand. Arms only shoulder width apart, but fingers open wide.

Skill Activity

Tuck jumps on the hands as illustrated should be featured very frequently in the early preparation classes. In order to maintain good balance the stomach muscles and top of pelvis must be pulled towards the lower spine, shoulders and hips in line with the hands.

Competition to see who can stay in this balance position the longest is a valuable activity for class teaching. Transferring weight from one hand to another will give strength and awareness.

Skill

The swing into handstand can then follow. The hand placement on the floor with no angle between body and arms is important, i.e. body and arms in straight line. The step into the handstand must be sufficiently forward to allow this. The body must lean forward over the thrusting leg which is bent before stretching and thrusting. The backward leg swings upwards to the inverted position, the thrusting leg following after the thrust. The shoulders must move forwards slightly in front of the hands during the thrust but move back into alignment when the handstand is in balance. The head must be in normal alignment with the spine.

Constant and continual practice must follow: balancing on benches, low beams and low bars, box top etc; changing the shape of the legs, wide straddles, stag position, i.e. one leg bent and one leg straight, both legs bent etc. Move about on the hands, walking forwards and back-

Tuck jumps.

Checking the shape of the handstand.

Handstand practice for transference to Beam. The wide box top will give confidence. Begin with the tuck jump.

The straddle jump into the handstand.

The legs rotating after the straddle in order to walk forward through a forward bend of the back.

The 'elephant lift'. Practise in two's. First the piked position weight forwards on the hands; then the leg lift through a wide straddle; and the handstand.

Lydia Gorbik of U.S.S.R.

wards; turning round on the floor — called 'pirouettes'. Move in and out of the handstand from and to different positions: from knees to knees; from straddle stand etc:

Time spent on the hands can never be too long. Being familiar and happy in that position will ensure success especially when performing the handstand on the Beam and Asymmetric Bars.

THE HANDSPRING

Progressive Learning Skills

1. During the warm-up and preparation time in class teaching, include this exercise for shoulder awareness, and by shoulders, I mean the whole shoulder structure of the upper back. In the standing position, take the arms upwards close to the head, shoulders down, not 'shrugged'. Now lift the shoulders and upper back with a dynamic explosive movement and return to normal stance but with the arms still raised. Repeat ten times.

2. Progress with this same practice. Stand sufficiently close to a wall for the body to lean slightly when the hands are on the wall supporting you. Shoulders should be normal. Press and thrust from the hands extending the upper back in order to push away from the wall and return to standing position. It is this action of extending the upper back and thrusting from the hands that will achieve the jump and assist in the handspring.

3. *Jumping from the Hands to the Handstand Position.*

Approach the jump through the handstand technique. Increasing the forward lean of the body, hands placed well in front of the thrusting leg, chest well forward over that leg. When the hands make contact with the floor, thrust, keeping arms absolutely straight — keep the body in complete tension throughout. The hips should lift upwards, stomach muscles contracted. The legs must be straight. The jump from the hands should occur just before the body reaches the inverted position and when the hands return to the floor the handstand in balance should be achieved.

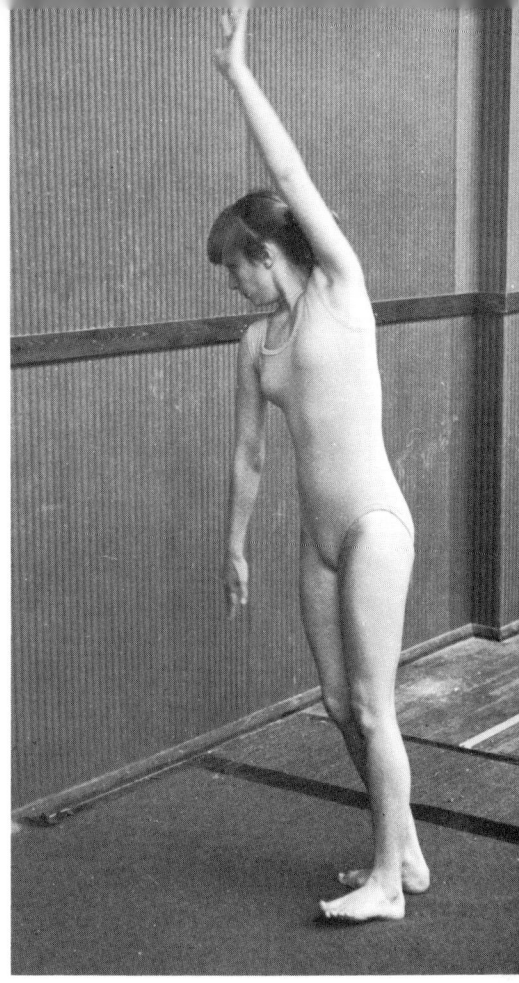

Shoulder and arm thrust activity for the handspring.

The same thrust is used for vaulting and this activity helps the technique of the handspring full twist from the top of the horse.

Jumping from the hands — this activity must be perfected before attempting the skill. The photograph shows the long step forward and the body well forward over the thrusting leg.

The Skill

The handspring is the jump from the hands, but in order to make a full rotation from the hands to feet, the speed of the leg swing must be increased and the thrust from the hands very vigorous and thrusting backwards over the head, arms straight and close to the head. Avoid taking a long run into the movement. Begin with two or three running steps. (Later and as the gymnast becomes stronger the handspring can begin by jumping from two feet at the same time swinging the arms from downwards to forwards and upwards.) Step forward out of the jump, leaning forward over the thrusting leg as in the handstand. The arms must be straight during the movement. The shoulders must not be above the hands until the thrust occurs. The leg swing must be fast and the thrusting foot must keep contact with the floor until the leg is straight. The hips must lift and the swinging leg must extend upwards. The thrusting leg should catch up with the swinging leg midway between the vertical and the landing on two feet.

THE HANDSTAND TO BRIDGE
Skill Activity

1. Begin in the back lying position, feet flat on the ground with the knees bent so that the feet are close to the seat. Hands placed behind the shoulders flat on the floor, fingers towards the feet. Lift the body from the floor until the arms are straight, increase the pressure through the feet until the legs are straight. This will extend the shoulders and upper back. Return to lying position.

2. From the tuck jump action, move the hips forwards over the shoulders bending the lower back and stretching the legs downwards to the floor into the bridge. Do not allow the shoulders to move forwards in front of the hands during the transition from tuck to bridge.

The bend following the extension to stand.

The extension in the shoulders.

The long stand into the handstand.

The Skill

From the balanced handstand, the shoulders must extend and move away from the direction of the movement. The body must not sag but retain the extended stretch. The upper back will arch as a result of the extension at the shoulders, and the body will begin to lower towards the ground, and the bend will continue down the spine. Allow the knees to bend only when contact is made on the floor with the feet. Keep the hips high, contract the seat muscles and push from the floor with the hands to the standing position.

THE BACK FLIP

Skill Activity

1. Push to the bridge from the back lying position, but bring the feet closer to the hands to allow a 'rocking' movement to occur from hands to feet. As the movement 'rocks' towards the hands, continue to thrust through the legs and feet sufficiently for the legs to lift and extend parallel and horizontal to the floor. Repeat three or four times in class lessons.

2. Working in groups of three, as in the illustrations on Page 38.

The bridge position showing the rocking action forwards towards the feet.

The leg thrust and lift to the horizontal position.

Working in groups of three, bend backwards keeping the head in line with the body.

Bending backwards to the bridge position.

The leg thrust into the handstand.

Bringing the feet down close to the box.

The vigorous leg kick aiming to coordinate the thrust from the hands as the legs swing downwards.

The swing into handstand.

Gymnasts should be of compatible size. The supported activity is through a back bend to the bridge with immediate thrust from two feet, legs extending and lifting up to the handstand position, followed by a thrusting downward of both legs to the ground. Arms lifting forwards and upwards over the head to the standing position. Support with one hand across back and one at the back of the thighs.

3. Donkey Kick or Leg Thrusting Action for the Back Flip. Using one section of a box — or a bench. Place the hands on the apparatus and kick to handstand. The handstand must reach the vertical position

39

with the stomach muscles contracted. Flex at the knee joint allowing the bend to continue until the heels are almost touching the backs of the legs. At that moment, drop the chest by hollowing the upper back momentarily. This will give an angle in body and arms in order to assist the thrust from the hands. The thrust from the hands is made simultaneously with the 'leg kick'. The legs must stretch and 'snap' downwards towards the floor, feet flat and close to the apparatus. The angle in body and arms extending in the thrust, arms lifting forwards and upwards strongly to a stretched position behind the head. Repeat many times.

STANDING BACK FLIP WITH SUPPORT

The gymnast begins in the standing position, arms overhead. The coach supports with both hands, one across the lower back with the hand stretching to the front of the body and on the pelvis, the other on the nearside thigh and just under the buttocks. The hand on the pelvis should guide the direction of the lean into the thrust, which must be backwards. The hand on the thigh should assist the leg thrust and the hip lift and extension.

The gymnast, from the standing position, must lean backwards off balance and at the same time bend at the ankles, knees and hip joints in order to immediately extend and thrust through the legs and feet into the backward flight on to the hands. Keep the head in line with the spine but take the arms back beyond the line of the head. The legs should remain straight, passing through the handstand position to 'snap' down as in the Donkey Kick practice described earlier. The hands must thrust from the ground swinging forwards and upwards over the head as the standing position is reached.

FORWARD AND BACKWARD WALKOVERS

These acrobatic type skills should not rely solely upon the gymnast's ability to bend in the spine. As in all gymnastic skills, there must be extension and amplitude. Pay particular attention to the legs — there must be a complete split of the legs throughout the movements.

Swetlanova Grossdova of the U.S.S.R. showing incredible mobility in her walkover across the beam.

Skill Activity

1. To assist the last part of the walkover, stand with back facing a beam or wall bar such that one leg lifted backwards can rest on the beam, heel upwards. Stand squarely with hips in alignment. Bend at the hips until the chest is close to the supporting leg. Now lift the body slowly to the upright position, arms in line with head. Hold for three seconds. Repeat five times.

2. As before, but facing the wall bar or beam. With one leg supported at hip level forwards bend backwards as far as you can without falling over then lift the back up again to the standing position. This will give you the 'feel' of the standing action out of the forward walkover.

3. A practice for the shoulder and leg extension in the backward walkover.

Place the hands on the floor, lift the appropriate leg high behind, place only the ball or toes of the supporting leg on the floor, both legs straight and wide apart. Extend the angle between body and arms by taking the chest towards the supporting leg and at the same time extending the legs still wider apart. Stretching the muscles at the back of the leg, lower the heel slowly to the floor. Press through the hands and arms, lifting the back upright to the standing position without allowing the free leg to drop downwards.

THE FORWARD WALKOVER

Begin as for the handstand. Do not allow the forward thrusting foot to lose contact with the floor until the full split of the legs is achieved. As the first leg reaches the floor the body must not 'sag' but lift by pressing through the hands and arms keeping the hips and free leg high. As the body reaches the upright position the stomach muscles should contract and the arms should be high in line with the head — eyes focused straight ahead.

THE BACKWARD WALKOVER

Begin in good standing stance with the arms high in line with the head. The bend must be in the spine — *do not displace the hips* — take the shoulders backwards, keeping the head in normal alignment and continue to bend from the upper spine through to the middle spine, the swinging or free leg should begin to move away from the supporting one as the bend begins. Again the supporting leg should not lose contact with the floor until the full split is achieved. The thrust or pressure of the supporting foot must be sufficient for the leg to keep as straight as possible before lifting and of course when moving through the walkover, the legs must be absolutely straight. A point of balance should be felt in the handstand position. The landing leg should be 'placed' on the ground, not 'dropped' to the ground, and the extension of legs and arms should be full, as described in the Skill Activity No. 3.

THE FREE WALKOVER

Skill Activity

Working in groups of three — supporting the gymnast with both hands; hand to hand and the other on the upper arm, at each side. Begin by thrusting vigorously with the take-off leg which is first bent, knee well forward over the toes, then straightened. The body must pike at the hips, chest well forward over the thrusting leg. The free leg must swing backwards through full splits. This action should be sufficient to start the rotation. Elevation is determined by the strong thrust and the swing of the free leg. As the thrusting leg leaves the floor, the body must extend and open out, keeping the hips high and legs wide as in the walkover action.

The Skill

The movement can then be attempted without support, but with the take-off from a Reuther board, landing into a soft mat. The arms must now assist the rotation by a strong downward and backward swing. When sufficient height is achieved, take away the aid of the Reuther board. Support may also be given by placing one hand on the pelvis and one in the lower back.

The first cartwheel — a tuck jump around the hands in support.

A free cartwheel being practised on low padded be[am]

Cartwheel using both hands and a guide line.

One-handed cartwheel. Either hand may take the we[ight]

THE CARTWHEEL

Skill Activity

1. Tuck jumps — taking off from one leg and placing hands one in front of the other on the floor. The jump will move in a half circle pattern on the floor.

2. Using a low bench or box top, take the weight on the hands, pushing from one leg followed by the other in a back scissor kick action over the apparatus.

3. Supporting the Cartwheel
Standing behind your partner, cross your arms right over left to support at the waist of a gymnast's right hand approach to the cartwheel. The approach step must be long with maximum bend at the knee. The body must move sideways and lean into the line of direction. The first arm must stretch out beyond the first leg and take the weight as the thrust begins from the first leg. The free leg must swing away from the thrusting leg, keeping the full split position. The second arm is kept up by the side of the head ready to take the weight as the turn begins — hands taking the weight alternately as the body 'wheels' sideways. The cartwheel must travel along a straight line and the body should keep a correct stance in the sideways plane.

The Skill

The cartwheel is exactly as described above. The wheeling action must be smooth and the legs controlled in order that a second cartwheel may be performed in sequence and without extra steps.

THE FREE CARTWHEEL

Skill Activity

Working in two's. Stand behind the performer and follow her movements through a cartwheel with the same support as for the cartwheel, but testing your ability to actually lift her a few inches from the floor as you support. This will give the gymnast the sensation of the free movement.

Alternatively, support can be given with one hand on the shoulder and one on the thigh.

The Skill

When the cartwheel action is well controlled, the free movement may be attempted alone. The thrust must be strong and sustained, and the legs must swing with force. The technique of the thrusting leg is the same as for the free walkover. A very strong thrust from this 'step in' leg, and a full splits of the free leg. The arm action must swing downwards and backwards to assist the rotation. As in the Free Walkover, a Reuther board can be used during the learning stages.

The Asymmetric Bars

Preparatory work for this piece of apparatus should be confined to a single bar. Either the low bar of the asymmetrics; one bar of a set of parallel bars; or a low horizontal bar. The last two pieces of apparatus are conventionally men's equipment. The height of the single bar can be adjusted to suit the physique of the gymnasts, but also to suit the movements being performed. In other words, the single bar can either be the low or the high bar of the asymmetrics.

Exercises on the asymmetrics must be made up of swinging, circling, springing and support elements, with changes of direction, flight movements, and turns. Each element described in the basic section will be classified for your guidance.

CARE OF THE HANDS

Magnesium Carbonate is necessary to use sparingly on the hands to dry the perspiration and therefore avoid any loss of 'grip'. Hand protection by means of thin leather straps is necessary for the elite gymnast but not for children in general class activities. The leather hand strap will reduce the friction on the palm of the hand, and will extend training time. Proficient gymnasts suffer less from blistered hands as they are capable of releasing and replacing the hands, whereas the beginner tends to grip tightly all the time. Should the hands blister and become sore, then an antiseptic cream must be used. Hard skin which forms as a result of continuous work on the bar must be treated with a pummice stone or a very fine piece of sand paper wrapped round a short piece of broom handle. Rotate the improvised 'sander' in the palm of your hand and sand the hard skin away.

BASIC SKILL ACTIVITIES ON SINGLE BAR FOR CLASS TEACHING

1. *Swinging*

Hands in ordinary grasp, swing forwards and backwards. Keep the arms straight and swing the whole body to a near horizontal position. Attempt to release the hands and recatch at the end of the backward swings.

2. *Half Turns*

When the swing is fluent and the body is reaching the horizontal, release one hand to make a half turn toward the hand still grasping the bar, and regrasp after the turn to continue swinging. Hands will now be in mixed grasp. If you have learnt to release and regrasp then at the end of the swing and as you recatch after the turn you can change the hand back to ordinary grasp. A valuable practice is to continue to make half turns on every other swing all along the length of the bar.

3. *The Underswing Shoot*

The Basic Underswing is, in this form quite simple, but the movement when developed will produce some of the most advanced skills to be performed on this piece of apparatus. Therefore, much attention should be paid to its performance, and the early inclusion of the basic underswing in the class activity is essential. Begin by standing at arms length from the bar and grasp in ordinary grasp. Place one foot slightly forward and the other foot backwards off the ground. Press against the bar with the hands, keeping the arms straight and at the same time swing the free leg forward. Allow the shoulders and upper body to fall backwards and the feet and hips rise up to, under and beyond the height of the bar in a hyper extension position of the body. Chest extending during the last part of the underswing thrust the arms and hands in an overhead action away from the bar to a standing position the other side of the bar.

4. *Piked Hang Position* — Hanging

From a hanging position on the bar, pass both legs bent between the hands. Keep the seat in line with the feet as you straighten the legs. The

The hand positions — ordinary grasp.

Mixed grasp.

Basic swinging on a single bar — note the release of hands.

Legs to be straight on the forward swing. Aim to swing to the horizontal.

Swinging with half turns, creating a mixed grasp of the hands.

Preparation for the underswing.

The underswing.

body should be piked, head in line with the spine. Hold the position for three seconds. Allow the feet to reach for the floor the body circling between the arms. Look for the floor, release grasp and stand up.

5. *Chinning the Low Bar* — Strength

This activity is very suitable and useful for the young class members. Two or three children at one time can use the bar for this simple strength exercise. Hands in ordinary grasp, pull the body upwards towards the bar by bending the arms and the *legs*. Hold the position for two seconds and return to stand.

6. *Back Pull-Over*

From one or two feet jump and pull on the arms to circle the bar backwards to front support.

7. *Mill Position*

Hands in reverse grasp — straight arms — legs extended.

8. *Backward Circle from Ground* — Circling

From standing position, hands in ordinary grasp, feet under the bar. With slight bend of the knees thrust downwards with legs to jump up, stretching the legs, keeping the arms straight and pressing downwards with the hands. Immediately 'tip' the body upside down, that is allow the shoulders to go backwards and the feet and hips to lift upwards, keeping the bar close to the hips. Pike at the hips very slightly keeping the bar close to the body. Continue to circle the bar, lifting the back upwards from under the bar and 'shifting' the hands to the top of the bar. Come to a front support position.

The lift of the back during the last part of the circle is significant, for later, when learning the Hecht or 'Eagle' catch, this action will aid the skills' success.

9. *The Lay-out* — Support to Swing

From the front support position slight bending of arms, pike at the hips, shoulders forward and legs forward under the bar. Immediately push down

The piked hang. 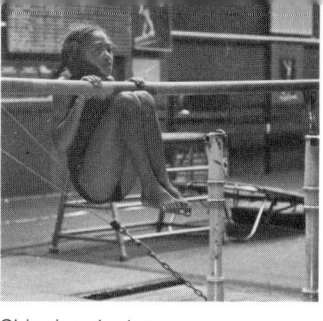　　Chinning the bar. 　　A back pullover. 　　Front support.

Mill support — the hands are in reverse grasp ready for a forward circle.

Swinging the legs forward under the bar in preparation for the lay-out.

The lay-out.

vigorously with the hands until the arms are straight, swinging the legs backwards and lifting the body from the bar. Keep the shoulders forwards and the stomach muscles contracted, pushing forwards on the bar to increase the angle between body and arms. Aim to lift the body to the horizontal position. Return to the front support by moving the shoulders forward, lowering the body back to the bar and piking into the bar on contact. Repeat this exercise three times.

10. *Lay-out to Handstand*

Support can be given at the shoulder and thigh. More shoulder and arm strength is required for this skill.

The piked underswing. Lydia Gorbik of U.S.S.R.

11. *The 'Float'* – Swinging

The 'Float' is the preparatory swing made before the 'Upstart', which will be described later. This skill activity should be included in the class teaching. It does not require support; it is vital for increasing strength in the legs and stomach and a very important action in the upstart.

Stand at full arm stretch away from the bar. Pike at the hips until the back is in alignment with the arms and parallel to the floor, the body and legs forming a right angle. Hands in ordinary grasp. Bend the knees in order to thrust downwards and backwards through the feet to lift from the floor, the body moving backwards before swinging forwards under the bar and extending at the hips to a stretched hang – returning again in the swing to the starting position. Keep the legs straight throughout the forward and backward swing.

12. *Squats and Straddles* – Springing

Place three or four sections of a box in front of the single bar. The box needs to be of a height to allow the bar to be level with the gymnasts' hips. Stand on the box with hands in ordinary grasp on the bar. Rise on the toes, preparatory to bending the knees and ankles in order to jump from the feet. During the bend of the legs, extend the angle between body and arms by a pulling action away from the bar. As the legs stretch for the take-off, pull the bar towards the hips, shoulders forwards over the bar and press downwards with the hands. Lift the hips and tuck the legs close up to the chest, squatting over the bar to the ground. Thrusting from the bar as the body passes over.

In the same way the straddle vault over the bar can be performed. Legs must move quickly and straight to a wide stretch and join again after passing over the bar.

13. *The Handstand from a Jump*

In the same way a handstand can be achieved. Jump into the handstand through a tucked position. Place a crash mat in front of the bar. If you reach the handstand, wheel out or overthrow to dismount. Progress to straddle up to the handstand in the same way as you perform the movement on the floor, but take the shoulders forward a little more and during *(far left)* Preparation and support method for the swing to handstand.

(left) The Handstand.

(below left) The swing back before the underswing.

(below right) The underswing (often referred to as the 'Float').

the lift into the handstand, press the bar away from you in order to increase the angle between the body and arms, thus achieving the handstand.

These ten single elements are a vital part of any gymnast's training. Until these are mastered and performed with good style, one cannot hope for progression. Yet all these activities can be taught without supporting the gymnast, therefore, they are ideal for a class lesson programme. Always be sure that the matting under the apparatus is sufficient to cushion any falls that may occur.

The time taken to achieve these skills will be considerably shorter if at the same time the gymnast has a programme of strengthening, mobility and tension exercises. Practise the following exercises or similar ones for ten minutes each day.

(above) Using two or three layers of a box to aid the first squat through to the ground.

(above right) In the same way the straddle over is attempted.

Passing through the handstand to overthrow to the ground.

Learning the handstand. First the preparation for the jump.

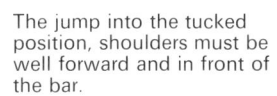

The jump into the tucked position, shoulders must be well forward and in front of the bar.

BASIC DAILY PROGRAMME IN STRENGTH, MOBILITY AND TENSION

1. *Five Chins* to the bar — body at full stretch, feet clear of the floor. Pull and bend the arms until the chin is level with the bar. Do not swing the legs about or bend at the knees.

2. *Five Leg Lifts* — body at full stretch, feet clear of the floor. Lift the legs straight by flexing at the hips until the toes touch the bar.

3. *Hip Mobility* — Long sitting on the floor, legs parted a little wider than shoulder and body width. Flex at the hips and press the chest to the floor — back quite flat. Arms stretched forward.

4. *Upper Leg and Arm Strength* — Long sitting on the floor, legs a little wider than in the previous exercise. Place the hands on the floor between the legs, taking the weight of the body to lift from the floor in the straddle position. Hold for three seconds and repeat three times.

5. *Stomach Strength* — Lying on your back at full stretch. Lift the legs six inches from the floor, keeping them straight. Hold for three seconds and repeat five times.

6. *Tension* — From a prone position on the floor, with hands and feet supporting body straight from head to toes. Contract the muscles of stomach, seat and legs and keep that position of tension for 20 seconds.

7. Lying flat on the back. Arms stretched overhead, legs together and straight. Contract the stomach muscles and press the middle spine to the floor. Raise the legs slightly, also the head, shoulders and arms, narrowing the chest and hold that position for ten seconds.

Now to move on to a slightly higher level of single bar skills for the smaller groups of elite gymnasts. These skills will only be achieved if there is some strength in arms, shoulders and stomach and tension in the body.

THE BACKWARD CIRCLE

From the front support position, swing the legs forward under the bar, bending the arms slightly and taking the shoulders forward. In other words, the basic preparation for the Lay-out. Lay-out to a horizontal position and, keeping the body in tension, bring the hips back to the bar, taking the legs forwards and the shoulders backwards. Head in line with the body. Press the bar into the hips and continue to circle once round the bar to front support. The hands of course must also circle the bar. Repeat the exercise three times. Do not allow the legs to 'drop' under the bar after each circle.

THE FORWARD CIRCLE

From the front support position — arms fully stretched and hands pressing down hard on the bar so that the bar is on the upper thighs. Extend the chest and hold the head in good alignment with the spine. Contract the seat muscles. Begin the circle by overbalancing forward, but do not collapse. The legs must move backwards. Almost immediately, and when the body is inverted, flex at the hips, moving the hands under and then on top of the bar as the body continues to circle now in the piked position. Keep the pike position until the shoulders are well forward in front of the bar as in the starting position, with the body piked, arms bent in readiness for the downward thrust of the hands and the lay-out of the body into the next element. This could be a:—

SOLE CIRCLE

This is compiled of the very basic actions of the lay-out, straddle position and the underswing.

    The feet are placed on the bar, outside and close to the hands after the lay-out. Keep the hips high and the shoulders forward in front of the bar into the pike position for the straddle on. Circle the low bar by pressing down with the balls of the feet against the bar, and pulling with the arms.

The forward circle begins in the front support position.

The legs will now begin to swing into the lay-out.

The body is now piked with the hands moving round the bar.

The lay-out.

(above right) The Sole Circle — note the feet are together and between the hands. They can however be outside of the hands.

(middle and bottom right) The one and a half twist from sole circle.

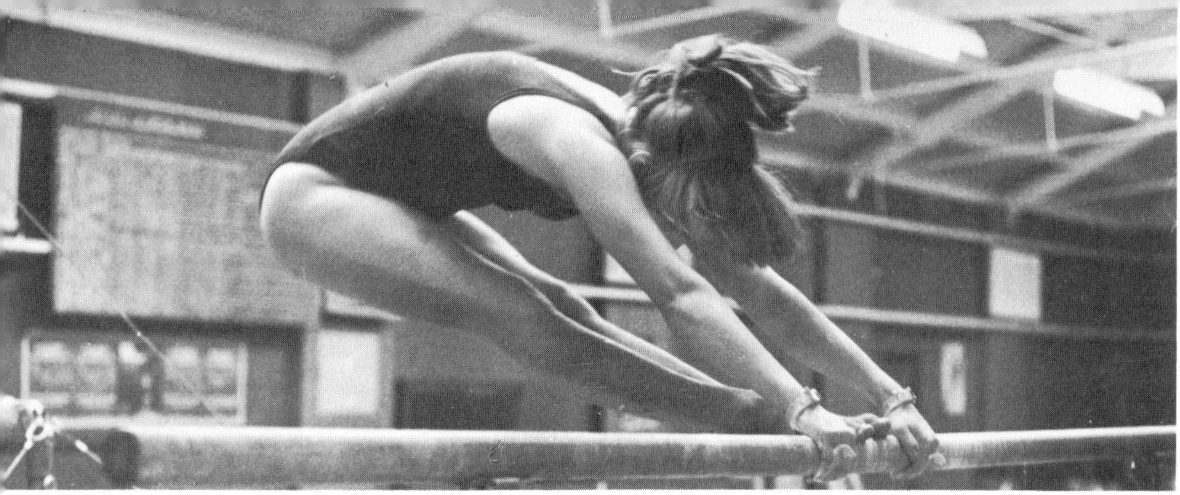

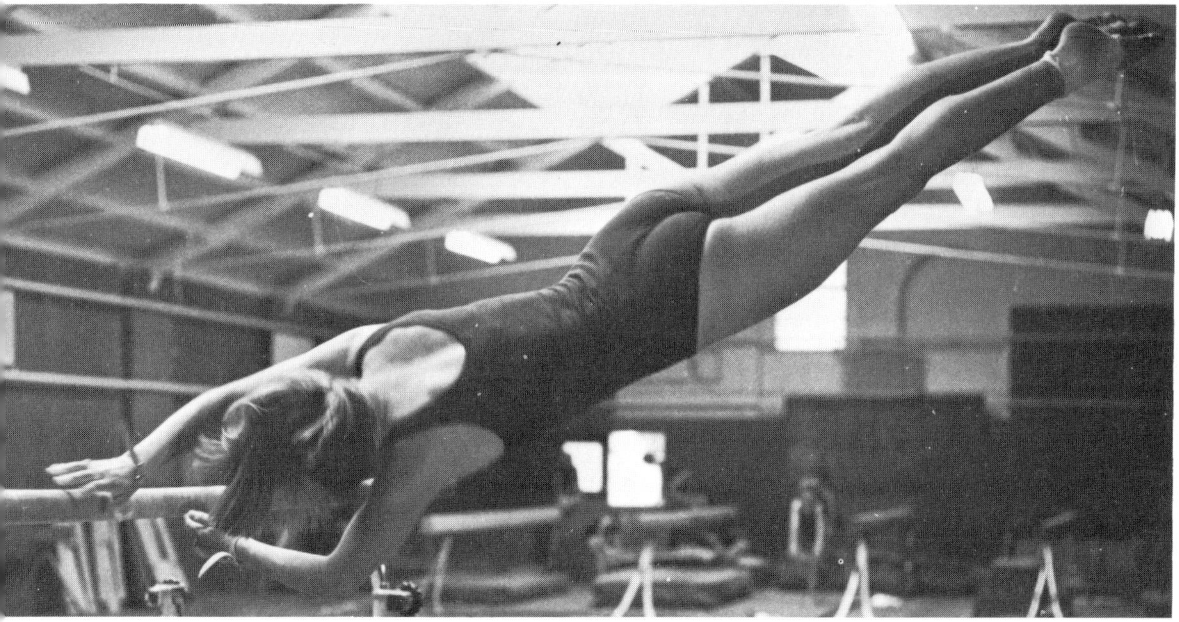

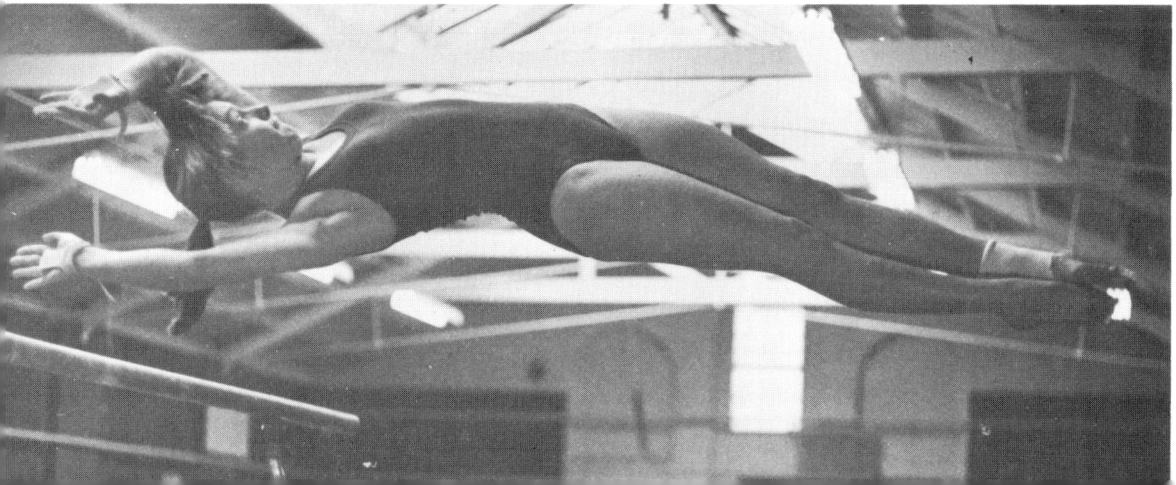

Ludmilla Turischeva performing the one and a half turn after the Sole Circle.

Keep the hips stretched away from the bar in the circle, chest close to thighs. Release the feet when the hips are horizontal and the circle is almost complete. Feet must continue to rise above the level of the bar, the body must extend with the chest opening and lifting as the hands thrust away from the bar, arms stretched overhead to dismount.

This movement need not be confined to the performance on the low single bar. It is very versatile. Add a half turn at the height of the underswing, releasing and regrasping the hands again on the turn to continue swinging. The skill can be performed on the high or the low bar and can begin facing either direction to swing into or to hip beat the lower bar. Eventually and in its very advanced form, it is the foundation for the Underswing with One and Half twists!

FORWARD SOLE CIRCLE

Begin as for the Backward Sole Circle. Lay-out and straddle on to the bar. The hips must be directly above the bar. As the circle begins, the hands must change to a reversed grasp. When the circle is threequarters round, the feet will release and swing forward into the float action. Hands again release and regrasp in ordinary grasp.

THE UPSTART

Skill Activities

1. I have already described the 'Float' or underswing action. Aim to swing to the horizontal, with full extension through arms and body.

2. Using a broom handle, lie flat on your back on the floor, arms stretched overhead and touching the floor, broom stick grasped in each hand, shoulder width apart. Lift the legs and hips and bring the feet to the broomstick. Press down with the hands, keeping the arms straight, moving the bar down the full length of the legs to the thighs and then to the hip joint. This action should cause the shoulders to lift from the floor and the legs lower to the sitting position. Repeat the action ten times.

The Broom Handle activity — this position is as the 'float'.

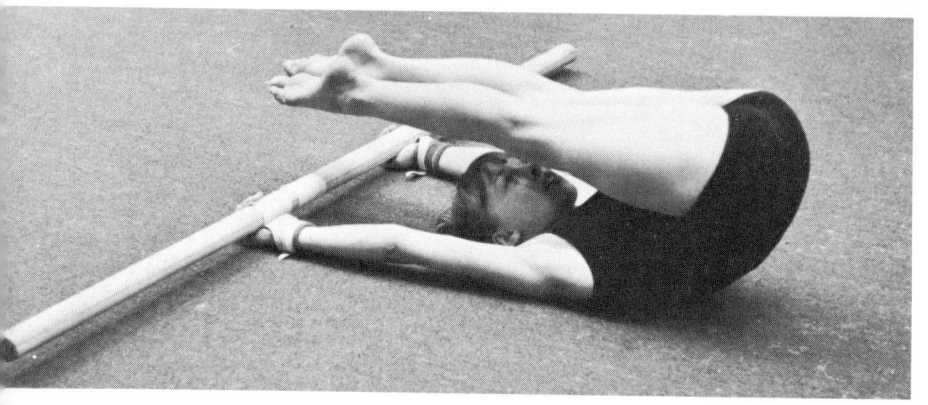

'Bringing the toes to the bar'.

Pressing the bar to the thighs.

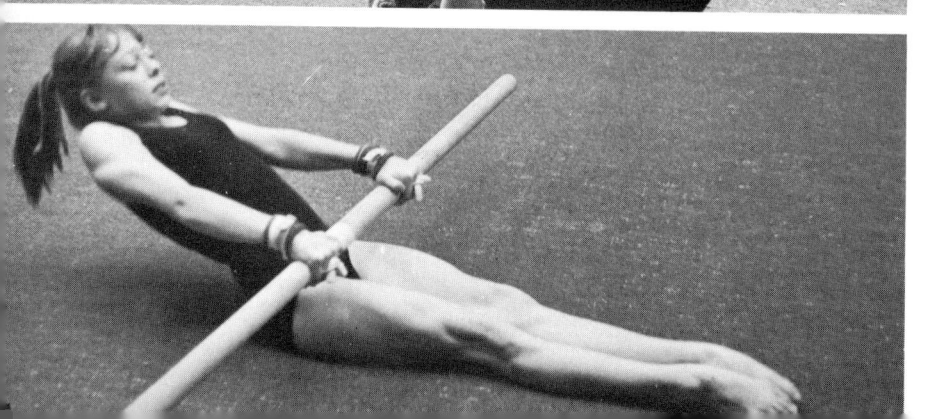

The shoulders moving forwards over the bar.

The first position for the upstart. Practise with the aid of the box.

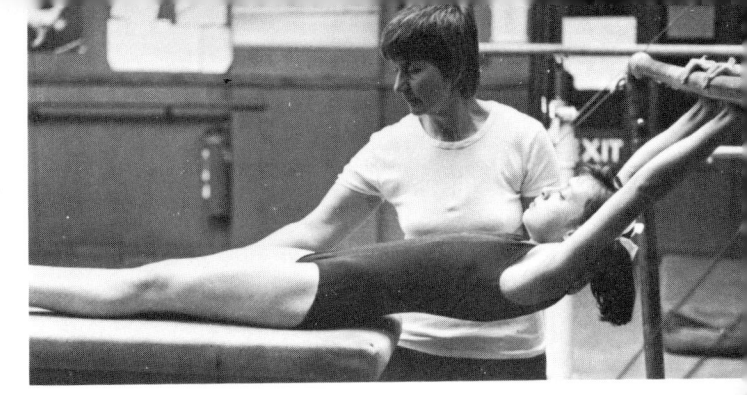

The pike by bringing the feet to the bar.

Pressing the bar downwards and taking the legs upwards.

Pressing the bar into the hips.

3. Place three layers of the box lengthways in front of the low bar at a suitable distance to enable the gymnast to lie at full stretch with legs and lower back only supported. The pike, with toes to the bar should be achieved whilst the back remains in contact with the box. Repeat the pike action five times. Now with support at the thighs and lower back, pike and take the toes to the bar. The legs must move quickly. Extend the feet and legs beyond the height of the bar. At the same time press downwards and backwards with the arms closing the angle between body and arms, to bring the bar into the hips. Moving the shoulders forwards and pressing downwards on the bar, swing the legs backwards into a horizontal lay-out. In this activity the upstart technique is being achieved even before the gymnast has strength in the body sufficient to precede it by the float.

The Underswing (Float) and Upstart

Having practised all the skill activities, (1) the underswing, (2) the broom handle action, (3) the upstart from the box top, and provided the body has been prepared sufficiently, the whole skill should not be difficult.

The vital points to remember are:

(a) The underswing must be full stretched
(b) The pike must be dynamic
(c) The hips must RISE as the pike is made
(d) The legs must continue to move up and beyond the height of the bar after the pike
(e) The bar must be pressed down and taken close into the hips.

The Upstart between the Bars

This has the same technique. The Underswing is substituted by the back hang, in support. The hips must keep near the bar and lift. Do not allow the shoulders to move backwards under the bar during the pike.

For strength and endurance, practise ten or twenty repetitions after your training session. Perform with rhythm and continuity by laying out after each upstart, taking the shoulders backwards and the feet forwards to swing under the bar to return to the back hang support.

The Long Upstart from High Bar

Again this has the same technique as in the upstart action. The stretched body swing can come from sitting, squatting or standing on the low bar facing the high bar, or from hip beat and swing over the low bar.

The extended swing should aim to lift and stretch to a near horizontal position to the floor as in the Underswing Upstart.

When this vocabulary of skills on the asymmetric bars has been successfully achieved with good style together with the ability to link the individual skills together into short sequences, then you will be ready and competent to attempt some of the more complex and exciting movements that can be evolved from these basic skills. Do not be in a hurry to advance, for invariably an advanced skill fails because the basic skill has been poorly executed or not sufficiently understood. Time spent on individual skill learning can never be too long, but nevertheless as soon as possible link movements together with continuity. Even on the single bar, one can compose sequences that will have immense value in the preparation of the final and full routine.

Examples of short sequences for the low bar

A.
1. Backward circle from standing to front support
2. Forward circle
3. Backward circle
4. Straddle on, backward sole circle undershoot with half turn to dismount.

B.
1. Long underswing and upstart
2. Straddle on, backward sole circle and underswing with half turn
3. To long underswing and upstart
4. Forward circle
5. Straddle on and forward sole circle
6. Release and long underswing upstart
7. Squat over bar to dismount.

There are many more single bar skills and many more sequence combinations. The B.A.G.A. Development and Competition Plan Booklet contains six progressive exercises, and is an excellent guide to the standards required for competition.

SKILLS FOR THE ASYMMETRIC BARS

Upstart to Catch

Begin as for the long underswing upstart and virtually complete the movement, that is, until the bar has reached the thighs. Continue to press downwards, thrusting from the hands to 'jump' and grasp the high bar. The legs must not be allowed to drop until the high bar is caught and the body must be elevated in the thrust.

THE LONG SWING WRAP TO EAGLE CATCH

Skill Activities

The descriptive title must be translated to be understood. The movement consists of a swing out from the high bar, swinging forwards to circle backwards around the low bar, at the same time releasing hands, which do not re-grasp until the body extends in an 'Eagle' shape to catch the high bar.

1. Skill Activity – 'Catch' Practice

Working in threes, two gymnasts holding a bar or broomstick 18 inches to two feet from the floor. The third gymnast lying face downwards so that the bar is level and above her middle back. Keeping legs and seat muscles contacted, arch the back, spreading the arms wide (as Eagle wings), rotating the wrists inwards in order to catch the bar. Hence the 'Eagle Catch'.

2. Skill Activity – Lift from Low Bar

From a hip hanging position on the low bar and with arm support around the legs and hand support in the ribs. The gymnast must lift the back vigorously, arms spread wide to grasp the high bar. Wrists must be rotated inwards in order to catch the bar.

A good long swing must be achieved.

Method of support for the first back lift to catch.

The gymnast must be capable of circling the bar after the long swing.

The back lift must be vigorous with the hips staying close to the bar.

The 'catch' practice, again with a broom handle or bar.

The 'catch' — body extended, arms high.

Suzanne Dando of the Ladywell Club — in competition.

3. Skill Activity – Long Swing

The lay-out and swing away from the high bar to circle the low bar can be approached first with the swing alone. The lay-out from the high bar must be horizontal with shoulders over the bar. Push the bar away from the body as it swings downwards, chest narrow, stomach and leg muscles contracted to produce a straight body swing. As the body reaches and makes contact with the low bar, the hips must flex and the legs swing upwards with the bar held in the hip joint. Keep the hands in contact with the high bar. Perfect this movement by repetitions. The width of the two bars is critical for this type of activity and adjustments must be made to suit each gymnast.

The Skill

When each skill activity has been mastered then the whole skill can be practised. The first attempts must be made with support from the coach. As in the back lift action from the low bar, the support must be around the upper legs and seat, second hand coming into the rib cage as the body leaves the bar.

The swing down is made as in activity (3). The legs must be upwards with the bar held in the hips before the hands are released from the high bar. The backward circle of the body continues, the arms stretching and held close to the head until the hang position of activity (2) is reached. The legs, however, must not be loose and hanging. The seat muscles must be contracted and the legs held in position. The back lift must be vigorous and the hips must stay close to the bar. The arms are lifted high and then spread wide to catch the high bar. Take the movement fairly gently, it does not require too much speed or force, and with crash mat in position the initial falls cause no problems.

THE 'TUMBLE TURN'

Skill Activities

1. From a long hang on the high bar, swing forwards and backwards. When the swing is strong, press down with the arms, closing the angle

The long swing.

Andrea Loughton of the Ladywell Club showing excellent technique.

The drop to catch the low bar.

between body and arms on the backward swing, lifting the legs upwards and wide apart, bringing them close to the body in an acute pike. Hold the position whilst the swing travels forwards, keeping the pike and lifting the seat towards the high bar. Open out and repeat.

The Skill

The Tumble Turn is really a somersault between the bars, but it is one of the simpler types, with very little 'flight'. However, it has a high tariff rating at present.

The approach may be made from *(a)* a long swing, *(b)* an upstart to catch, or *(c)* a squat between the arms. The technique of the movement is the same and as described in the skill activity. The piked turn must be kept close to the high bar and the pike maintained to enable the transition to the low bar to swing through to the float and upstart and not drop with force. The shoulders must be above the low bar at the moment of release and the feet must be directed towards the low bar.

THE RADOCHLA SOMERSAULT

This somersault is more difficult than the 'Tumble Turn', so called because the first gymnast to perform the skill was an East German gymnast named Bridgette Radochla. The advance in women's gymnastics skills has now produced the Comaneci Somersault — very similar, but requiring more skill and confidence since it is performed from the high bar to the high bar and therefore is a complete 360° turn in flight.

Skill Activity

From front support on low bar, facing outwards, lay out to the horizonal, thrusting very hard from the hands in order to flex at the hips, lifting the seat to the level of the top bar. Keep the head in line with the arms. Repeat many times.

The preparation for the strong hip lift to the high bar.

The hip lift.

Supporting the Radachla Somersault.

Ruth Adderley of the Ladywell Club in competition.

Nadia Comaneci of Roumania performing for the first time by any gymnast a Radochla from high bar to high bar!

The Skill

There should always be a crash mat under the bar during the training of this skill and in competition the mat should be at least two inches in depth. With support, two coaches in the first attempts, stand either side of the gymnast and support with one hand on the upper arm and one on the upper leg. Guide the gymnast's arm between her legs to the high bar and support the leg into the lay-out. The gymnast must thrust downwards very strongly with the hands, pushing forwards before releasing to take her arms between the legs to catch the high bar. Keep the pike acute during the turn, opening the body and swinging the legs backwards after catching the high bar. When more confident, have one coach supporting only by guiding and support at the upper leg.

THE HECHT DISMOUNT

Skill Activity

You will need two crash mats in front of the low bar or single bar. It is also wise to wear your tights or tracksuit trousers as the constant attempts when learning, chaff the front of the legs.

From front support, bring the legs forward under the bar and the shoulders forwards, creating an acute pike of the body, arms slightly bent. The action is a jump or thrust from the thighs. The body must pike in order to gain and initiate the thrust. It is a good idea to have support at each side with the first attempts. Supporting firmly at the arms, allow the gymnast freedom to take the arms downwards with the pike of the body and then assist as she attempts to thrust from the bar. The thrust contact comes from high up on the thighs. The very strong and dynamic body lift

Support methods for the first attempts. The back lift must be strong and the body held in good tension throughout.

Swetlanova of U.S.S.R. A straddled hecht from a clear circle — perfect and beautiful.

An attempt to Hecht!

to extension and the contraction of the seat and leg muscles creates the thrust.

The first attempts will probably sprawl on the crash mats, but as the action is felt and the confidence grows, the Hecht will be achieved.

The Skill

The Hecht can be performed from
(a) Backward hip circle to Hecht
(b) Short clear circle to Hecht
(c) Long swing and back hip circle.

The Simple Hecht

From front support, lay-out to the horizontal and backward circle of the bar. When the body is piked as in the skill activity, the action of lifting the back vigorously and extending the body will lift you from the bar. Keep the legs and body in tension, extending the arms forwards in the flight to dismount.

Long Swing to Hecht

This movement is a combination of the long swing and backward hip circle as in the Eagle catch, but in the Hecht, the swing forwards of the legs must be strong and vigorous to the wrap action. The sustained pull of the hands on the high bar, together with the 'wrap' of the hips, will depress the bars and as the holds release, the reaction in the bars will assist the 'jump' from the thighs. The body must retain its tension especially in the back and seat. The flight from the bar must be upwards.

Support for this skill must be given in the base of the spine as the body is wrapping the bar, and under the rib cage in the flight off.

There are, of course, many more skills to the asymmetric bars. I have space only to describe a few. But intelligent understanding of the basic techniques will enable the good coach to see that half and full turns, release and catch actions will, if added to the basic skills, produce many more advanced movements.

Vaulting

In order to have success with this section of gymnastics, whether you are performing at a high or a low level, the gymnast must be able to run fast. The whole essence of the vault is in the approach and the take-off. If these two actions are weak, then nothing spectacular will be achieved.

Running each day should become a habit for the elite gymnast. One mile in the local park or even around the street block is essential, both for the success of the vault and for general fitness and stamina of the gymnast.

The running action must be as a sprinting athlete. Knees forward, legs extending in the drive, arms assisting by pushing forwards and backwards close to the body.

For the sport of gymnastics, we are only concerned with two basic vaults for the beginner. The Squat and the Straddle. When they can be performed well with flight and good control, then progression can be made to the handspring types.

In this section I am only going to describe the skill activities and the aids to progression.

CLASS ACTIVITIES

1. Bench and Mat – Arm swing practice

From a standing position about one foot from the bench, bend the knees and take the arms backwards to a low position behind the body. Spring upwards and over the bench from two feet, swinging the arms forwards and upwards on the jump. Land in a controlled manner, knees and ankles bending slightly on landing, stomach muscles contracted, arms upwards

Activity for helping the technique of the vigorous upward body thrust.

The same thrust from the board. This position is a little low on the board.

The upward flight, a good activity for all abilities.

Progressing the activity — jump to either land onto or over the low box.

First flight activity, showing how to support.

by the side of the head. Press the heels to the ground, straighten the knees, bringing the arms down to the sides to stand erect.

Skill Activities

Arm swing and take-off practice

2. **Reuther Board and Mat.** From a short run of about five or six paces, jump from the board with two feet together, extending legs, body straight, arms swinging from down behind to forwards and upwards in the flight. The arm swing is very important. It must be correct at this stage and in this simple activity. It is very essential in the advance vaulting action that the arms come from behind and swing through with a strong lift upwards to assist the jump and strike out for the top of the horse.

Board take-off practice

3. *Reuther Board, one section of a Box and Mat.* As before and from five or six paces, run fast and jump from the board to clear the box, landing on the mat. The body must be fully extended in flight, arms as before, swinging from behind to stretch upwards.

Landing practice

4. *Horse or Box (3 or 4 layers) and Mat.* From a standing position on the box, with arms behind the body, swinging them forwards and upwards, jump upwards with extended body and legs to land in a controlled position on the mat. Bring the legs slightly in front of the body in flight in order to land in balance.

Squat Vault — Beginners

5. *Horse or Box, Mat and Reuther Board.* From six or eight paces, run fast and jump from the board to swing the arms forwards to shoulder height and place them shoulder width apart on the apparatus. Lift the hips and squat the feet between the hands. Immediately extend the legs and thrust from the feet swinging arms upwards, to extend the body in flight and land in a controlled manner on the far side of the apparatus.

THE SQUAT VAULT – Competition Level

Having had experience in all the previous activities, the first attempts at the Squat vault for competition level should be quite competent.

Begin with eight to ten paces, running fast. The run, when calculated according to the board position and length of paces, must be measured, that is, the distance from the starting position to the jump on the board must be known to the last inch or centimetre. This run must be constant when all else is finally established, and the distance of the board from the horse is correct for your take-off. The gap between the board and the horse should ideally allow the gymnast to have full extension in body and arms after the take-off and before reaching the horse, but, of course, this will depend upon the speed and power of the approach run and take-off, and also the courage of the gymnast.

During the first flight, the body must be full extended before the tuck, and should not rise above the horizontal.

The thrust from the horse must be vigorous and immediate. The chest and shoulders rise with the thrust in order for the body to extend again before landing. Second flight should have equal lengths to first flight.

HANDSPRING TYPE VAULTS Skill Activities

1. The 'Handstand – Jump' from the hands as described in the acrobatic section of the book is a very essential practice for vaulting.

Second Flight Action

2. Using two horses or boxes, one placed crossways to form a 'T' shape. The gap between the two should be adjusted to suit the height of the gymnast. From a standing position on the box which is lengthways, make an approach as for handspring. The position of the forward leg on the lengthways box should be such as to allow the gymnasts shoulders to be well before the hands (as in photo). Hands are placed on the crossways box. The chest must be close to the forward and thrusting leg.

The action is that of the handspring, but without any pre take-off action, simply a step in as in the jump from the hands. The aim of this activity is to improve the second flight and landing. The body should

Supporting to get the feel of the straight second flight.

The body angle is correct for achieving good second flight.

The landing.

The landing is flat on the back to help the straight body technique.

Laura Wynne showing good flight technique.

Showing support in first flight.

A second board to help the very small gymnast and young!

Learning to twist in flight — a safe activity for all.

N.B. All photographs show skill activities essential for confidence-building in vaulting as well as good technique.

straight in the air. The thrust should bring you to your feet. Do not allow the back to bend. Support in the back and shoulder helps to 'feel' this straight position in the air.

You can, of course, practise half and full turns in flight from this 'safe' situation.

Overswing practice

3. *Reuther Board, one layer of a Box and Crash Mat.* With five or six paces, approach the board in the normal way. The board should be at least one metre away from the box. Jump from the board with correct arm swing and lift the legs fast from the board into a tucked position with straight arms, and immediately thrust from the box to land in a straight back drop action, or onto the feet.

When the sensation of turning over on the hands is familiar and the thrust from the hands is strong with straight arms, then the board must be placed at a suitable distance to allow the first flight to have a straight body and extended leg action. Land in a straight back drop action, arms overhead.

4. In order to gain confidence for the final stage of the handspring vault, we can use yet another skill activity.

Place four or five benches parallel to each other in order to make a platform. Place two or three crash mats on top so that the height is around three feet six inches or one metre ten centimetres. Approach the apparatus in the same way as in skill activity (3). Aim to have the arms straight when contact is made with the top of the mats. Land in a straight back drop action, flat on the mats, arms overhead.

This activity with the soft, large landing area is ideal and very essential when learning the twisting vaults.

The smaller gymnasts may use two Reuther boards one on top of the other to assist the take-off either in this skill activity or when vaulting over the horse.

Support can be given to aid the first flight and to give confidence. The coach stands between the board and horse and guides the flight with

Christine Cullers of the Ladywell Club in training – The Long Arm Overthrow.

support in the hips. When the action is correct and the gymnast has confidence, then the transition may be made to the horse.

The performance of the handspring vault must be perfected before progress is made to twist or pike the body whilst in flight, either in the first or second flight phase.

Remember that the essence of good vaulting is good running. Do not neglect your daily running training.

Second flight – Laura Wynne.

The Long Arm with full twist – Suzanne Dando.

The Beam

The essential physical requirements for performing on the beam are correct body alignment during all movements which must include acrobatics as well as dance steps and balances. Good body tension and strong back muscles, and above all, one must be completely CONFIDENT.

Body alignment and control must be understood and practised from the first lesson. The ballet and the preparation exercises will produce this awareness. If this poise and balance is not apparent when working on the floor, then it will be very difficult to make any progress on the beam.

Many hours must be spent walking along the beam and turning at each end on the balls of the feet to gain confidence. Progress to running, then jumping, full turns, kneeling and sitting positions. Be happy moving along the beam. When you are, then you know you have sufficient confidence to try the more difficult elements.

Always during the learning and training of new movements and especially of the acrobatic types, the first attempts must be made on the floor, then the bench, then the low beam, and then the beam at a height of three or more feet. Unless your cartwheel can be performed on a straight line on the floor, it certainly will not be successful on the beam. When progressing to the high beam for the first time to try your new advanced skill, have plenty of soft mats to cushion any falls that may happen. Have the coach standing by if necessary, but remember, if the coach has virtually to lift you through the movement, then you are certainly not ready to try it. If, too, you have to stand on the beam for more than a few seconds, plucking up courage to go, then again you are not sufficiently prepared.

Handspring practice on padded benches.

Back-flip — this skill must be performed with confidence on the bench before taking it to the beam.

The same preparation must be given to the back somersault.

The next progression for the back somersault – pack the crash mats under the beam and straddle the legs to land on the mats in your first attempts.

The last four photographs show the back somersault from take-off to landing – Andrea Loughton of Ladywell Gymnastics Club, the first girl in Great Britain to perform this skill in competition.

These four photographs show the incredible poise, control and skill of Nadia Comaneci of Roumania during the Olympics at Montreal in 1976.

Nellie Kim of U.S.S.R. showing correctness of the basic stance for the beam.

A typical training session at the Ladywell Gym Club.

Suppleness and balance — Swetlanova Grossdova of U.S.S.R.

The low benches must be used constantly for the perfecting of the advanced movements and also of the series of movements; such as two backward walkovers without stopping; a cartwheel back-flip; or two free forward rolls, etc.

Never try to perform any movement on the beam unless you are absolutely sure that you can perform it well and with confidence on the floor.

Beam exercises may contain almost any movement that can be performed on the floor. The exercise must be composed of a variety of different types of movements, not all acrobatics and not all dance. The exercise should have originality and continuity. The exercise should not have stops for the preparation of a movement. The ideal exercise should have fluidity, slow and fast movements, movements performed at different levels and a variety of skills from all categories.

Beams are now made with padded covers which are assisting and making popular the somersaults and all free flight skills.

The beam is one of the most difficult and unpredictable pieces of apparatus. Do not scorn it, but treat it with respect and spend as long as possible with and on it. In this way you will begin to enjoy beam work and be successful at it.

CONCLUSION

In conclusion, may I say to coach and gymnast alike — enjoy your sport — it is a wonderful one — but work hard at the basics and the advanced skills will take care of themselves.